MAJOR UNSOLVED CRIMES

Crime and Detection series

- Criminal Terminology
- Cyber Crime
- Daily Prison Life
- Death Row and Capital Punishment
- Domestic Crime
- Famous Prisons
- Famous Trials
- Forensic Science
- Government Intelligence Agencies
- Hate Crimes
- The History and Methods of Torture
- The History of Punishment
- International Terrorism
- Major Unsolved Crimes
- Organized Crime
- Protecting Yourself Against Criminals
- Race and Crime
- Serial Murders
- The United States Justice System
- The War Against Drugs

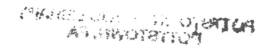

CRIME AND DETECTION

MAJOR UNSOLVED CRIMES

BRIAN INNES

MASON CREST PUBLISHERS
www.masoncrest.com

Mason Crest Publishers Inc.
370 Reed Road
Broomall, PA 19008
(866) MCP-BOOK (toll free)
www.masoncrest.com

First printing

1 2 3 4 5 6 7 8 9 10

Library of Congress Cataloging-in-Publication Data on file at the Library of Congress

ISBN 1-59084-382-7

Editorial and design by
Amber Books Ltd.
Bradley's Close
74–77 White Lion Street
London N1 9PF
www.amberbooks.co.uk

Project Editor: Michael Spilling
Design: Floyd Sayers
Picture Research: Natasha Jones

Printed and bound in Malaysia

Picture credits
Amber Books: 66, 72, 74; Corbis: 11, 12, 13, 14, 15, 16, 17, 18, 24, 32, 33, 35, 39, 40, 42, 64, 68, 71, 83, 84, 85; PA Photos: 8; Picture Desk, Kobal Collection: 76; Popperfoto: 28, 29, 81, 89; SMG Newspapers Ltd: 44, 45, 46, 47, 49, 50, 53; Topham Picturepoint: 6, 22, 27, 30, 34, 36, 54, 56, 57, 58, 59, 60, 63, 70, 78, 86; TRH: 67.
Front cover: Corbis (main and center right), Topham Picturepoint (bottom left).

CONTENTS

Introduction

From the moment in the Book of Genesis when Cain's envy of his brother Abel erupted into violence, crime has been an inescapable feature of human life. Every society ever known has had its own sense of how things ought to be, its deeply held views on how men and women should behave. Yet in every age there have been individuals ready to break these rules for their own advantage: they must be resisted if the community is to thrive.

This exciting and vividly illustrated series of books sets out the history of crime and detection from the earliest times to the present day, from the empires of the ancient world to the towns and cities of the 21st century. From the commandments of the great religions to the theories of modern psychologists, it considers changing attitudes toward offenders and their actions. Contemporary crime is examined in its many different forms: everything from racial hatred to industrial espionage, from serial murder to drug trafficking, from international terrorism to domestic violence.

The series looks, too, at the heroic work of those men and women entrusted with the task of overseeing and maintaining law and order, from judges and court officials to police officers and other law enforcement agents. The tools and techniques at their disposal are described in detail, and the ethical issues they face are concisely and clearly explained.

All in all, the *Crime and Detection* series provides a comprehensive and accessible account of this exciting world, in theory and in practice, past and present.

CHARLIE FULLER

Executive Director, International Association of Undercover Officers

Left: Here, Richard John Bingham, seventh Earl of Lucan, prepares for a flight. Lord Lucan was a notorious gambler and playboy who mysteriously disappeared following the murder of the family's nanny, Sandra Rivett, in London, England, in 1974.

The Disappearance of Jimmy Hoffa

His name was James Riddle Hoffa, and a riddle is what he left behind him. There is little doubt that he has been dead now for nearly 30 years, but what became of his body and how he died remains a mystery. On July 30, 1975, Jimmy Hoffa, ex-president of the Teamsters Union, left his home at Lake Orion, saying he was going to a meeting. He told his wife, Josephine, to whom he had been married 39 years, to expect him around 4.00 P.M., because he would be grilling steaks for dinner. But he never returned.

THE MAKING OF A UNION MAN

Jimmy Hoffa was born in Brazil, Indiana, on February 14, 1913, the son of a coal miner who died of lung disease in 1920. His mother (from whom he took his middle name) took in laundry. He later said she was a woman "who believed that duty and discipline were spelled with capital Ds." In 1922, the Hoffas relocated to Clinton, Indiana, and two years later, to Detroit.

Jimmy dropped out of school in the ninth grade in 1929. A friend advised him to try to get work in the food industry ("Whatever happens, people have got to eat"), and he found a job unloading railroad cars and trucks for the Kroger Grocery & Baking Company.

Conditions were hard, and the foreman was a harsh disciplinarian. One

Left: James Riddle Hoffa was vice president of the powerful Teamsters Union when he was called before a Senate inquiry, the McClellan Committee, in 1957, to testify against charges that he had made improper use of union funds.

night in the spring of 1931, two of young Hoffa's workmates were fired for going to a food cart for their dinner, and he called for a work stoppage just as a load of strawberries arrived. The company was forced to negotiate before the fruit deteriorated and perished, and within days, Hoffa had secured union recognition, as Federal Local 19341 of the American Federation of Labor. The following year, he took on the job of full-time organizer for the International Brotherhood of Teamsters, taking the Kroger union with him.

THE UNION BOSS

Hoffa's rise to presidency of the Teamsters was a long and hard struggle. During the 1930s, union organizing was a difficult and often dangerous activity. Employers hired tough strikebreakers and called in police to disperse strikers' pickets. Hoffa later described it, saying, "Our cars were bombed out. Three different times, someone broke into the office and destroyed our furniture....Your life was in your hands every day. There was only one way to survive: fight back. And we used to slug it out on the streets....The police were no help. The police would beat your brains out for even talking union. The cops harassed us every day. If you went on strike, you got your head broken."

In his first year as Teamsters' organizer, he was beaten by police or strikebreakers 24 times; and he said that he had once been arrested 18 times during a single 24-hour period of picketing: "Every time I showed up on the picket line, I got thrown in jail. Every time they released me, I went back to the picket line."

These early experiences made Hoffa into a ruthless, uncompromising, negotiator with a single-minded, driving ambition. Inevitably, he found himself operating more and more on the fringes of the law as the power of the Teamsters—and that of Hoffa himself—increased. In the late 1950s, a Senate inquiry, the McClellan Committee, began looking into improper labor practices, and a convicted **racketeer**, John Dioguardi, alleged that

Long before the Teamsters Union became powerful, labor relations in the United States had a history of violence and intimidation behind them, as shown by this photograph of a picket line of dockers, with its dangling noose as a threat to strike breakers and non-union workers.

The Senate charges against Hoffa could not be proven, but the Teamsters' president, Dave Beck, was found guilty of embezzlement and tax evasion. Here, in October 1957, Hoffa is carried shoulder-high by his supporters after winning a landslide election to replace Beck as president.

The Caucus Room in the Senate Office Building, Washington, D.C., was packed with observers in August 1957, when Hoffa commenced his testimony before the McClellan Committee's inquiry into racketeering within the Teamsters Union.

Hoffa, now vice president of the union, had made use of union funds for his own profit, as well as accepting payoffs from trucking employers.

HOFFA BECOMES THE UNION'S PRESIDENT

The charges were never proved, however, and in 1957, Hoffa was **acquitted** of a charge that he had attempted to bribe one of the committee's investigators. The union's president, Dave Beck, was convicted on charges

The law finally caught up with Jimmy Hoffa in 1964, when a federal investigation led to him being found guilty of extortion, jury tampering, and conspiring to defraud the Teamsters Union's pension fund. Here, he is led from the court after his conviction.

of **embezzlement** and tax evasion, the Teamsters were expelled from the American Federation of Labor, and Hoffa became president in Beck's place.

The chief counsel to the McClellan Committee was Robert F. Kennedy, who was not satisfied with this result and vowed that he would continue to pursue the Teamsters' boss. In his 1960 book, *The Enemy Within*, Kennedy described the union as a "conspiracy of evil." Hoffa found himself the target of federal investigators, accused of violence, fraud, and continuing misuse of union funds. When Kennedy became Attorney General in his brother's

Jimmy Hoffa gained an enemy in Robert F. Kennedy, who described the Teamsters Union as a "conspiracy of evil," and determined to pursue his investigations. A typical confrontation between Hoffa and the young Kennedy, at that time a senator, during a racketeering inquiry in 1958.

THE MOB CONNECTION

Hoffa never attempted to hide his connections with Detroit gangsters during his early career or later on with national mobsters. "These organized crime figures are the people you should know if you're going to avoid having anyone interfere with your strike....We make it our business, and the head of any union who didn't would be a fool. Know who your potential enemies are and know how to neutralize 'em." But his dealings with them undoubtedly made him many enemies.

Another confrontation between two bitter enemies at one of the Senate inquiries into racketeering: the young Senator Robert F. Kennedy, who later became Attorney General during the presidency of his brother John F. Kennedy, and Jimmy Hoffa. Hoffa's attorney, George S. Fitzgerald, keeps out of the argument.

administration, the pressure mounted. Finally, in 1964, Hoffa, charged in Nashville with extortion, was convicted of jury tampering and sentenced to eight years' imprisonment. Shortly afterward, he received a sentence of an additional five years, when he was convicted in Chicago of fraud and conspiracy in the handling of a union benefits fund.

After several appeals, Hoffa was at last committed to Lewisburg Federal Prison, but he refused to give up presidency of the Teamsters, and appointed Frank Fitzsimmons, the vice president, as "caretaker." Over the

Jimmy Hoffa strides angrily from court in 1975, after unsuccessfully appealing against President Nixon's ban forbidding him from union management until 1981. His attorney told the court that Hoffa had been "thrown out of prison," and that the ban was harsher than his original punishment.

next four years, his applications for **parole** were turned down; after he announced in 1971 that he was resigning the presidency, President Nixon **commuted** his sentence, but banned him from taking part in union activities until 1981. Hoffa returned home on December 23, 1971, determined to find a way to regain control of the Teamsters.

A MEETING WITH DEATH?

When Hoffa left his home on July 30, 1975, he told his wife he was bound for a 2:00 P.M. meeting with union members, along with underworld figures "Tony Jack" Giacalone and "Tony Pro" Provenzano (a Teamsters boss from New Jersey), at the Marchus Red Fox Restaurant in downtown Detroit. Relations between Hoffa and Provenzano had been cool since their time together in Lewisburg Jail, where Provenzano had also been imprisoned for racketeering and extortion. Hoffa blamed "Tony Pro" for the federal investigation that had resulted in his downfall.

On his way to the meeting, Hoffa stopped off at Airport Service Lines, a limousine company in which he was a secret partner with Louis "the Pope" Linteau, and told him of the forthcoming meeting. At 2:20 P.M., he telephoned his wife from the Marchus Red Fox Restaurant, complaining that no one had yet arrived. At 2:45 P.M., he was seen getting into a car in

THE FATE OF THE SUSPECTS

Tony Giacalone was sentenced to 10 years for tax fraud; he died in 2001, while under indictment for racketeering. Tony Provenzano died in prison while serving a life sentence for murder after his conviction in 1978. Salvatore "Sally Bugs" Briguglio was shot to death in New York, also in 1978. Jimmy Coonan was imprisoned for life in 1988. Louis Linteau died in 1978 of natural causes.

the restaurant parking lot, and Linteau later reported that Hoffa had called him at (he said) 3:30 P.M., saying "Tony Jack" had arranged a meeting, but had not turned up. Next morning, Hoffa's green Pontiac was found in the restaurant lot, unlocked. Of Hoffa, however, there was no further sign.

Giacalone and Provenzano both denied that they had fixed a meeting with Hoffa and were able to establish **alibis**. Giacalone had been at a barber's and then with his lawyer. Provenzano had been playing cards with friends in New Jersey.

On August 12, Hoffa's son, James Hoffa, Jr., received a ransom note. It was signed "Queen Liz" and demanded $1 million in small-denomination bills: "If law is around, goodbye James Riddle Hoffa. We send back nuts, not ears. He is already wounded, we had to cut him up a bit." The money was to be handed over at the 711 Bar in downtown Detroit, but only the police turned up. The car in which Hoffa was seen to leave the Marchus Red Fox was traced, and some of his hair and traces of blood were found, although there were no clues as to anyone else who had been in it.

Then, on November 5, Teamster Ralph Picardo, serving time for murder, contacted the FBI. He said two of Provenzano's friends had visited him in prison and had carelessly let slip that they had provided his alibi. However, a grand jury hearing got no nearer the truth.

WHERE IS THE BODY?

As for what happened to Hoffa's body, there were many underworld rumors. One mobster said that he had been **garroted** by "Sally Bugs" Briguglio at a syndicate hideout, after which his body was processed in a meat-grinding plant and the pieces thrown into a Florida swamp. Another story is that the body was enclosed in a 55-gallon drum filled with wet cement and dropped into the Gulf of Mexico. Then, in 1989, contract killer Donald "Tony the Greek" Frankos told *Playboy* magazine that a New York gangster named Jimmy Coonan had shot Hoffa. Hitman "Mad Dog" Sullivan had dismembered the corpse and kept the pieces in a freezer before burying them in an oil drum in the end zone of Giants Stadium in New Jersey. However, nobody has ever excavated the site to verify if this is true.

Hoffa was declared legally dead in 1982. His son, James Jr., became president of the Teamsters, and in 1995, he and Hoffa's daughter, Barbara, held a memorial service for their father in Detroit. More than 2,000 friends and former associates attended. The FBI, who amassed more than 70 volumes on Hoffa's activities, believes that the Mob killed Hoffa to prevent him from regaining his presidency. Conspiracy theorists, however, claim that he was murdered because he knew too much about the assassination of President Kennedy. Said his longtime friend Robert Holmes: "Everybody was mad at Hoffa but his membership. He was a real rank-and-file guy. The world has changed, everything has changed. I don't know if he could do now what he did."

ANOTHER SUSPECT?

Jimmy Hoffa was rumored to have had an affair, in the early 1930s, with a woman named Sylvia Pagano. Around that time, she gave birth to a boy, who took the name of Chuckie O'Brien, and looked remarkably like Hoffa, who treated him as a member of his family. On the day he disappeared, the Teamster boss was reported to have been driven away from the Marchus Red Fox in a maroon Mercury. That same day, Chuckie had borrowed a marron Mercury from "Tony's" son. In the investigation into Hoffa's disappearance, the FBI brought four trained dogs to the car; their handler claimed they found Jimmy's scent in the back seat and trunk. Chuckie later took the Fifth Amendment before a Detroit grand jury, as did "Tony Jack" and "Tony Pro." The FBI also found human hair in the car. In August 2001, they announced that DNA analysis had established this as Hoffa's.

Murder in the Bahamas

In 1943, Sir Harry Oakes was considered one of the world's richest men. He was born in Sangerville, Maine, in 1874 and—although destined for a career in medicine—was seized with the fever for gold prospecting at age 20. After many fruitless years—and countless adventures— searching throughout the world, he finally struck lucky at Kirkland Lake, Ontario, in 1913, and was suddenly rich beyond his wildest dreams. He married an Australian girl in 1917, took Canadian citizenship in 1924, and, after donating lavishly to many charities, was made a British baronet in 1939. However, in 1937, having received a tax bill for $3 million from the Canadian government, and following the advice of Harold Christie, a Bahamian property developer, he relocated to the tax-free islands of the Bahamas.

Early on the morning of July 8, 1943, his body was found in the bedroom of his palatial beach-front mansion in New Providence, battered to death and partially burned by a gasoline fire. The murder was discovered by Harold Christie, who was a guest in the house, and he immediately called Government House. Asleep in bed, the governor of the islands was none other than the Duke of Windsor—the former king Edward VIII of the United Kingdom, who had abdicated his throne for the sake of the woman who now lay beside him, the twice-divorced American, Wallis Simpson.

Left: A typical pose by Sir Harry Oakes, pictured with a machete on his estate in the Bahamas. After a wildly adventurous life searching for gold throughout the world, he finally found a rich seam in Ontario, married, and became one of the world's richest men.

In 1941 Oakes and a party of friends visited San Salvador. Photographed next to a monument marking where Columbus is believed to have landed are, from left to right, property developer Harold Christie, Oakes, his secretary, and Robert L. Ripley, of *Believe it or Not* fame.

INVESTIGATION AND TRIAL

The awakened duke immediately imposed a 48-hour blackout on the news. Then, rather than consulting the local police or New Scotland Yard in London, he telephoned Miami, and asked for two local detectives: Captain Edward Melchen, the head of Miami homicide, who had acted as the duke's bodyguard during a visit to Florida, and fingerprint expert Captain James Barker. It was later alleged that the duke had asked the detectives if they would "confirm the details of a suicide."

By early afternoon, the two detectives had flown to New Providence. They found that the murderer had apparently attempted to set fire to the house: gasoline had been splashed all around the bedroom and in a downstairs room, but the fire had not taken hold. Bloody handprints were on both doors of Christie's room—though he said that these were left after he had discovered Oakes' body. The stairs from the first floor were covered with mud and sand, and the traces of the footprints of several men—which were soon obscured by the crowd of sightseers that the Miami detectives let in—and there were scorch marks on the walls.

Among those who were able to visit the scene of the crime was Alfred de Marigny, a Mauritian-born French aristocrat, who had recently become Oakes' son-in-law after a secret marriage to his eldest daughter, Nancy. Captain Barker had omitted to bring his special fingerprint camera from Miami, but he was able to "lift" several prints from a Chinese screen beside Oakes' bed, and he subsequently established that one of these was of de Marigny's little finger. The two detectives examined de Marigny and claimed that they found singed hairs on his arms and in his beard and moustache—though guests at his house that night remembered that he had burned himself while lighting some candles.

Within 36 hours, de Marigny had been arrested for the murder. He had certainly driven past the house at the time the murder was committed, and relations between him and Oakes, following his marriage to Oakes' daughter, were well known to be far from cordial. However, at his trial four months later, the prosecution case rapidly fell apart. The two Miami detectives had failed to find the two nightwatchmen who were supposed to be on duty at the time of the murder, and who had disappeared. They had made no search for a murder weapon, and ignored the evidence on the stairs. And they were unable to produce photographs of the crucial fingerprint in court. The judge dismissed all of Barker's evidence, calling it "incredible for an expert," and de Marigny was declared not guilty.

Before the trial, and following de Marigny's acquittal, there were distinct signs of a cover-up. The Bahamas' Commissioner of Police, who had accompanied de Marigny when he first visited Oakes' bedroom, was suddenly transferred to Trinidad by the duke, and was unable to testify at the trial. An offer by President Franklin D. Roosevelt to provide the services of the FBI was declined. A watchman who said he had seen a mysterious motor launch land two men, and later take them off, on the night of the murder was "found drowned."

So who killed Sir Harry Oakes? More than 30 years after the murder, two books by American writers put forward a plausible theory that he had been killed by the Mafia. It is a complex story.

"JUSTIFIABLE HOMICIDE"

Sir Harry Oakes, it is claimed, was involved in smuggling gold to Mexico, using the yacht of Axel Wenner-Gren, a wealthy Swede who was known to be a Nazi sympathizer. The duke, desperate to find a way of financing his wife's extravagances, was drawn into the scheme. And the surveillance reports of the FBI on Wenner-Gren somehow managed to get into the hands of the Mafia, who used them to blackmail Oakes and Christie, as well as the duke.

The Mafia "associate" involved was Meyer Lansky, who had established a very successful chain of gambling casinos in Cuba. At the height of World War II, however, he was finding it difficult to attract sufficient tourist trade—"There weren't enough boats, and at that time, you didn't have enough planes… you can't live from the Cuban people themselves"—and turned his attention to the more accessible Bahamas.

Lansky sent a man called Frank Marshall (real name Francesco Castellianchi) to sound out Oakes and Christie—and, it is said, the duke himself. Oakes bluntly refused to have anything to do with the legalization of gambling in the Bahamas, but Christie—and the duke?—were terrified that their currency dealings would be uncovered. The Mafia decided that Oakes had to be persuaded.

Alfred de Marigny, Mauritian-born French aristocrat and Sir Harry Oakes' estranged son-in-law, is led from court during his trial for the murder. Due to evidence considered unsafe at the trial, he was found "not guilty." In 1959, the case was reopened, but the murderer was not identified.

Sir Harry Oakes with his eldest daughter Nancy, photographed in Florida in 1940. Her secret decision to marry Alfred de Marigny (at 34, twice her age) led to regular quarrels between the two men. At the time of the murder, she was on vacation with other members of the Oakes family.

On the evening of July 7, according to this story, Oakes was drugged as he sat drinking with Christie after dinner. Marshall arrived around midnight, and took the two men by car to a motor launch at the docks in

Nassau. There the question of a gambling license was once more raised. Oakes again refused to consider the possibility and lost his temper; there was a struggle, and he was struck over the head, fracturing his skull. His body was carried back to his home and Christie was told to go to bed—and then Marshall and his companions attempted to set fire to the house. It is further alleged that the duke was telephoned early next morning, and told which detectives he should bring in as investigators. It is certainly true that, when Captain Barker was shot dead by his son in 1952, it was declared "justifiable homicide"—he was found to have been in the pay of the Mafia for many years.

Nevertheless, it was not until 1963 (18 years after the duke had resigned as governor) that the Mafia obtained a casino license in the Bahamas. By 1983, the U.S. Drug Enforcement Administration estimated that 80 percent of illegal drug traffic into the United States came through the islands. Harry Oakes' mansion was demolished, and became the site of the Playboy Casino. And his killer has never been identified.

By all accounts, Harold Christie was a kindly man who did much for the the Bahamian people, helped develop the tourist industry, was a member of the Nassau House Assembly, and was knighted in 1964. Nevertheless, de Marigny's lawyer said of the murder: "I think Sir Harold knew more than he was telling."

The Black Dahlia

On the morning of January 15, 1947, two Los Angeles police patrolmen answered a call that a drunk had been sighted asleep in a deserted spot of wasteland. They found, not a drunk, but the dead body of a naked woman. To their horror, they discovered that the whole of her torso had been cut out and deposited a short distance away. The most striking fact was that there was almost no blood at the scene, and medical examiners soon concluded that the body had been cut apart elsewhere—and appeared to have been washed afterward. They suggested that it had possibly been placed in a bathtub. There were deep knife slashes on the corpse, burns made with a lighted cigarette, and the initials "BD" carved in the victim's thigh. Evidence indicated that these injuries had been inflicted while she was still alive. There was nothing to identify the body, so fingerprints were taken and sent to the FBI. They reported that the victim was Elizabeth Short, who had provided fingerprints when she was working as a government employee at Camp Cooke, a California Army training base, in 1942.

BETH SHORT

Elizabeth Short was born in Boston on July 29, 1924, the third daughter of a designer of miniature golf courses named Cleo Alvin Short. Her mother, Phoebe, later bore him two more daughters. The Wall Street Crash of 1929 and the subsequent Depression ruined Short's business. In 1930, he disappeared, and it was presumed he had committed suicide. Phoebe was left to bring up the five girls in poverty.

Left: Having set her sights upon becoming a Hollywood star, Elizabeth Short dyed her hair black and circulated promotional photographs such as this among the numerous "talent agencies" in Los Angeles. Instead, she ended up a dismembered corpse on a deserted patch of wasteland.

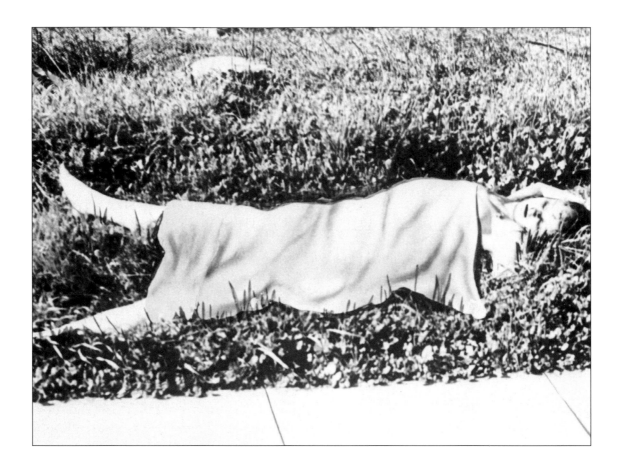

Covered with a blanket to hide the hideous dismemberment of her torso, the body of 23-year-old Elizabeth Short (at that time identified as "a girl of 16 or 17") was photographed where it was found, in a vacant lot on the southwest section of Los Angeles.

Like many young girls of the era, Elizabeth dreamed of becoming a movie star. In 1942, her mother was amazed to receive a letter from the missing Cleo, who was alive and living in Vallejo, California. Elizabeth, who suffered from asthma, decided that the Californian climate would suit her better than that of New England, and set out to find the father she hardly remembered. However, she and her father did not get along. He accused her of laziness and disapproved of the sailors with whom she spent her time. It was then that she found work as a civilian cashier at Camp Cooke and decided that, from now on, she would be known as "Beth."

Elizabeth, now Beth, was a popular figure among the soldiers, among whom she was once elected "Cutie of the Week." She had no regular

During the golden years of Hollywood, innumerable girls, like Beth Short, traveled westward in the hope of being "discovered" and achieving fame and fortune in the movie business. A good pair of legs and a dazzling smile were considered essentials for these budding "starlets."

boyfriend, but made many friends. It was when she was on a trip to Santa Barbara, on the coast, with a group of these friends, that she was arrested and charged with consuming alcohol while under age. She was sent back to Massachusetts, but, after a few months, returned to California. This time, she moved to Hollywood, where she roomed with a girl named Lucille. She was now determined to find work in the motion picture business and she and Lucille regularly hung out at the Hollywood Canteen, a gathering place for aspiring actors and agents.

BETH SHORT'S SECRET

But there was something unusual about Beth. A physically attractive young woman, she flirted charmingly with anybody she thought might help her

Elizabeth Short became engaged to dashing USAAF pilot Major Matt Gordan, whom she met in Miami, in 1944. The couple appeared very much in love, and Gordan gave Elizabeth an expensive gold and diamond watch. However, he was killed in a plane crash in India the following year.

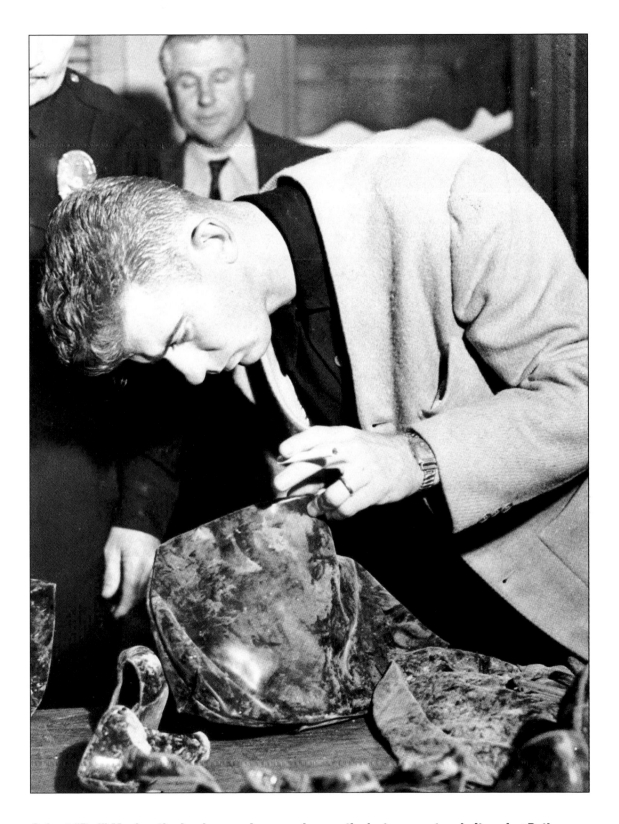

Robert "Red" Manley, the hardware salesman who was the last person to admit seeing Beth Short alive, was called in by police to identify a woman's purse that was found abandoned some distance away from her murdered body. He confirmed that the purse was indeed hers.

Inevitably, "Red" Manley was one of the first suspects in the "Black Dahlia" murder. He submitted to a polygraph (lie detector) examination a week after her death, and, when the test proved inconclusive, he was booked on suspicion. His wife, however, provided a firm alibi.

find a job in movies, including movie heartthrob Franchot Tone, but always finally rejected their advances. After her murder, the **autopsy** revealed the probable reason: she was not fully sexually developed.

Nevertheless, on a winter trip to Miami in 1944, Beth met a glamorous

GEORGETTE BAUERDORF

One of the girls with whom Beth became close at the Hollywood Canteen was Georgette Bauerdorf. One day, Georgette was found dead in her apartment. Clad only in her pajama top, she lay strangled in a bath of bloody water. Her bruised body revealed that she had struggled bravely before dying and had then been raped.

Georgette came from a well-to-do family, her father being a colleague of press baron William Randolph Hearst. The prime suspect in the murder, a GI with whom she was involved, was never traced. The Hearst family connection was used to suppress the publication of any details after the initial press reports, and this remains another unexplained murder.

USAAF pilot, Major Matt Gordan, and became engaged to him. He gave her expensive presents, but was shortly posted to India, and, in May 1945, she learned that he had been killed in a plane crash. It may have been mourning for her loss that led her, at this time, to begin dressing all in black, wearing tight-fitting black dresses, sheer black underwear, black shoes, and a jet ring. She dyed her hair black and wore pale, almost white, makeup. When she returned to California, this—and her custom of sometimes wearing a flower behind her ear—earned her the nickname of "The Black Dahlia," in reference to the newly released movie *The Blue Dahlia*, starring Alan Ladd.

For a year, Beth continued her attempts in the movie business, flirting outrageously with any man she hoped might help her, and moving from rooming house to rooming house. She met up with an acting coach, Lauretta Ruiz, and posed for some promotional photographs. Then, for a short time, she lived in the house of nightclub owner Mark Hansen, who allegedly offered her work as a stripper in one of his nightclub shows, the "Beautiful Girl Revue of 1947." After this, she followed a new boyfriend, a U.S. Navy officer named Lester Warren, to San Diego, but the relationship soon broke up. She began dating other men, and found refuge in the home of a movie usherette named Dorothy French.

Beth was picked up on a street corner in December 1946 by a tall, red-haired, hardware salesman named Robert Manley, whom she referred to as "Red." They dated once or twice, and on January 8, 1947, he called at the French home, at which point Beth asked him to drive her to Los Angeles. Her luggage was left at the Greyhound bus station, and he dropped her at the Biltmore Hotel. She did not take a room there, and, at 10 P.M., disappeared into the night. It was the last time she was seen alive.

AN INTENSE INVESTIGATION

The police investigation into Beth's murder was intense. From a list of friends' addresses provided by her mother and a scrapbook she had left in one of her former lodgings, they were able to piece together a history of the victim's movements. "Red" was found on January 20. It turned out that he was married, and his wife provided him with a watertight alibi for the night of the murder. However, he was able to give the police one small, although frustrating, lead. He had seen scratches on Beth's arms, and when he asked her about their cause, she said she had a friend who was "insanely jealous." He also identified a pair of shoes and a purse, discovered on a garbage dump, as hers.

The police brought in a number of suspects, subjecting some to brutal questioning, but were forced eventually to release every one. They were hampered in their investigation during the following weeks by an outbreak of sex killings that resembled the murder of Beth Short, but came to the final conclusion that these were "copy cat" crimes.

Another factor that obstructed the investigation was the number of false confessions they received. This often happens in the days following the

On February 5, former restaurant employee Daniel Voorhees signed a single-sentence confession: "I did kill Elizabeth Short." However, he was found to be intoxicated and too confused to take a polygraph test, and he was soon eliminated from the inquiry into her murder.

A MYSTERIOUS LETTER

On January 21, the offices of the *Los Angeles Examiner* received a call. It was impossible to tell whether the caller was a man or a woman. In a calm monotone, the caller gave details of the tortures that had been inflicted on Beth and promised to send "souvenirs" of the killing by mail. Three days later, they arrived in an envelope, addressed with pasted-on letters cut from newspapers: "Here! is Dahlia's Belongings Letter To Follow." The envelope contained a Greyhound left-luggage receipt dated January 9, Beth's birth certificate, her social security card, some photos and newspaper clippings about Major Gordan—and her address book, with one page ripped out.

Detectives questioned all those listed in the book, but each had an alibi. It seemed likely that the murderer had torn out the page that included his (or her) name. On January 27, the promised letter arrived at the *Examiner*. Once again, it was in letters cut from newspapers, and read: "Turning in Wed, Jan 29 10:00 A.M. Had my fun at police. Black Dahlia Avenger." Hoping that this meant the killer would give himself up, the police waited expectantly. But at 1:00 P.M., January 29, three hours later than the appointed time, they received a final note: "Changed my mind. You would not give me square deal. Dahlia killing was justified."

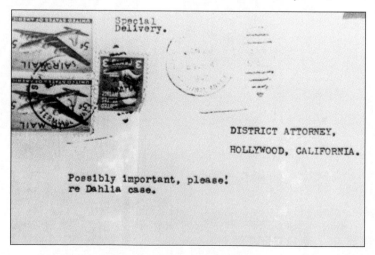

DISTRICT ATTORNEY,
HOLLYWOOD, CALIFORNIA.

Possibly important, please!
re Dahlia case.

publication of news of a murder, when mentally unbalanced people seek notoriety. However, it was the quantity of confessions that most disrupted police work. At least 40 people confessed to being the Black Dahlia's killer. One was a 33-year-old former restaurant employee, Daniel Voorhees. At police headquarters, he signed a statement that was then displayed to waiting reporters. It simply said: "I did kill Elizabeth Short."

However, Voorhees had been drinking, denied having written any letters to the *Examiner*, and was considered too "bewildered and befuddled" to take a lie detector test. He was held in custody—but as a mental case.

The investigation dragged on unsuccessfully for years. Then Detective John St. John received information on a likely suspect. A man known as Arnold Smith had said that he had been in the company of another man, Al Morrison, when he had murdered Beth Short. The information was on tape, and Smith described the killing in great detail. St. John could discover no trace of an Al Morrison and concluded that Smith was the real murderer. Smith was also known as Jack Anderson Wilson, who had been a suspect in the murder of a woman named Georgette Bauerdorf (see page 37).

THE MURDER REMAINS UNSOLVED

Although his whereabouts were not known, messages could be left for Smith at a cafe, St. John was informed. The informant agreed to leave a note arranging a meeting, and the police planned to pick up Smith there. However, on February 4, 1982, just days before the date of the meeting, Smith—drunk—set fire to his hotel bed with a lighted cigarette and burned to death. The District Attorney's office concluded:

"The circumstantial evidence is of such a nature that, were this suspect alive, an intensive inquiry would be recommended. And, depending upon the outcome of such an inquiry…it is conceivable that Jack Wilson might have been charged as a suspect in the murder of Elizabeth Short…."

And, with that final statement, the murder of Elizabeth Short, aka the Black Dahlia, remained unsolved.

Who Was Bible John?

Some time after midnight on February 23, 1968, a man living in a house in the city of Glasgow, Scotland, went to the garage at the rear of his home. Close by the garage door, he found the body of a young woman, naked, brutally beaten about the face and head, and strangled.

The problem immediately facing the police was the identity of the victim. There was no sign of her clothing, apart from a pair of high-heeled shoes. In fact, nothing was found to provide a clue. Wondering whether she might be a nurse from a nearby hospital, the police called members of the staff, but nobody recognized her. It was more than 12 hours later that a man named John Wilson, who lived only 100 yards away, identified the dead woman as his daughter, Mrs. Patricia Docker. She was married to a serviceman in the RAF and had been living at her father's home for a year, after returning from an overseas posting with her husband.

BARROWLAND BALLROOM

On the evening of February 22, Patricia had gone to a dance at the Barrowland Ballroom in the city, but police inquiries there provided no information as to whom she might have met there. Dragging a river that ran close by the place where her body was found resulted in the recovery of her purse, bracelet, and part of her watch. The police theorized that Patricia might have been murdered in a fit of rage by a man she could have refused to have sex with but, without witnesses or a single suspect to back the theory, they had to confess themselves baffled.

Left: In lanes behind grim tenement rows in Glasgow like these, the man who came to be known as "Bible John" left the stripped, beaten, and strangled bodies of his victims. Some 35 years have passed, but his identity, despite continuing investigation, has never been discovered.

Then, 18 months later, another woman was found murdered in the city, and certain aspects of the crime suggested that the murderer of Patricia Docker had killed her.

Jemima McDonald was a 32-year-old unmarried mother of three children. On the evening of Saturday, August 16, 1969, she had gone to the Barrowland Ballroom, as she frequently did, leaving her sister Margaret

The body of Patricia Docker, the young wife of an RAF serviceman, was found by the doorway of a garage in this back lane in the early hours of February 23, 1968. There was no sign of her clothing, apart from a pair of high-heeled shoes, and it was some time before she was identified.

The first known victim of the killer known as "Bible John," 25-year-old Patricia Docker. She had been dancing at the Barrowland Ballroom the previous evening, and her brutally beaten body was discovered only a few hundred yards from her father's home.

Dead woman's home

Block where body lay

Mackeith Street, Glasgow, where 32-year-old Jemima McDonald's body was discovered, close to her home. She had been killed in similar circumstances to Patricia Docker after leaving the Barrowland Ballroom with a tallish man described as auburn-haired and wearing a dark suit.

babysitting for her. She had told her sister that she might not return home until the next day, as she sometimes stayed out all night with friends, so it was not until Monday morning that Margaret became seriously concerned. When she overheard children talking about a body they had seen in a nearby derelict apartment block, she decided to see for herself and discovered, to her horror, Jemima's partly clothed corpse.

Within a few hours, some 100 police officers were assigned to a full-scale murder investigation. The autopsy revealed that Jemima had been savagely beaten before being strangled and, like Patricia Docker, she had been menstruating at the time of her death. This time, the police had a little more information. Jemima had been seen with a man at the Barrowland Ballroom at around 11:00 P.M. He was said to be aged 25–35, wearing a dark suit, and with auburn-colored hair, neatly cut. Jemima was seen again at 12:20 A.M., with a man answering to a similar description, and again 20 minutes later outside the building where her body was found. Police artists put together a sketch of the wanted man from the witnesses' descriptions. This was circulated to every police station in Scotland; some 70 people were questioned as possible suspects, but all were released without charge.

ANOTHER MURDER VICTIM

Two months after Jemima McDonald's murder, the police were no further along in their investigation. Plainclothes officers spent some time at dances at the ballroom, but the crowded dance floor gave them little chance of spotting the wanted man. Then, on the night of October 30, Mrs. Helen Puttock was

The body of 29-year-old Helen Puttock was found only 150 yards from her home. Unlike the previous victims, she was fully clothed, but had been strangled with one of her own stockings and sexually assaulted.

THE SEARCH FOR BIBLE JOHN

Armed with the similar descriptions of the presumed murderer of both Jemima McDonald and Helen Puttock, the police approached a leading Scottish artist, Lennox Paterson, deputy director of Glasgow's world-famous Art School. The sketch he produced was judged a good likeness, and many people reported that they knew the man, but all were different men.

More than 450 hairdressers were shown the sketch, with its distinctive style of hair, but none could identify him as one of their regulars. No dentist recognized the overlapping tooth. Some 5,000 men were interviewed during the first year of the police investigation; 70 looked like Paterson's sketch, and around a dozen were almost identical. Jeannie Williams herself viewed some 300 suspects, but did not recognize any of them. Nearing desperation, the detectives called on the services of the famous Dutch psychic, Gerard Croiset. He had proved helpful in a number of crimes, both in Europe and the United States, but he was unable to come up with any useful leads. The case remained unsolved. Then, in the 1980s, using the new technique of Videofit, the police took Paterson's original sketch and digitally "aged" it to produce an image of what he might look like after nearly 20 years. This, however, led to no further identification.

murdered in Glasgow. Age 29, with two young children, she—like Patricia Docker—was the wife of a serviceman. Her brutally beaten body was found in the backyard of a row of houses only 150 yards from her home. She had been strangled with one of her own stockings and sexually assaulted, but remained fully dressed. And, significantly, it was discovered that she, too, had been menstruating.

Much more could be learned about Helen's movements that night, because she had gone to the Barrowland Ballroom with her sister-in-law, Jeannie Williams. Both had found partners and had talked together. The two men were both named John, and Jeannie said Helen's partner seemed much more sophisticated.

When the two couples left the ballroom around 11:00 P.M., Jeannie's partner said goodnight and went off to take a bus, and the remaining trio hailed a cab. In conversation during the journey, said Jeannie, Helen's "John" said that he had had a strict upbringing and talked a great deal about

Some 100 police officers were involved in the investigation into the "Bible John" murders. Despite the circulation of artist's impressions of the wanted killer, and the interviewing of around 5,000 men, they came no nearer to identifying the killer.

Prominent Scottish artist Lennox Paterson, the deputy director of Glasgow Art School, produced this sketch of the wanted man, which witnesses considered a good likeness. However, although more than 450 hairdressers, and many dentists, were shown the drawing, none could identify him.

the Bible. It was this that soon earned the unknown man the name of "Bible John." Jeannie left the cab near her home, and Helen and her partner paid the driver outside the premises where her body was found. Jeannie was able to give a detailed description of the man presumed to be Helen's murderer. He was aged 25–35, 5 feet 10 inches to 6 feet tall, of average build, with auburn hair. He had blue-gray eyes and straight teeth, although one of the upper-right front teeth overlapped another. He wore a "brownish-flecked" single-breasted suit, a light blue shirt, and a dark tie with red diagonal stripes. His watch, she said, had a "military-style" strap: broad leather with a narrower strap running through it.

Five other murders of women took place in Scotland, all unsolved, in five months during 1977. Were these also the work of Bible John? It seems improbable that seven years should have elapsed before he reappeared, and the details of the killings were different. However, two possible suspects have been named as Bible John in recent years.

TWO SUSPECTS

In 1995, the police investigation into the Bible John murders was reopened. The development of DNA analysis made it possible to compare specimens from a sexually assaulted person with the DNA of a suspect, even if he is dead. Using a computer database, the police reexamined all the evidence gathered in 1969 and came up with a list of 12 men. And heading the list was the name of John McInnes.

John Irvine McInnes was born in 1938, in Stonehouse, a village to the south of Glasgow, his parents being fundamentalist Christians. He served two years in the Scots Guards and married in 1964. The marriage lasted only four years, however, and McInnes moved away from Stonehouse, returning occasionally to visit his mother. Despite his strict upbringing, he was a regular drinker.

At the time of the Glasgow murders, McInnes was a regular visitor to the Barrowland Ballroom. A fastidiously dressed man, he wore suits and his

Scots Guards regimental tie: dark blue with red diagonal stripes. He was, naturally, one of those interviewed by the police and attended four lineups without being recognized. Subsequently, he often referred to himself as "Bible John," quoting the Bible and apparently enjoying the role. On the evening of April 29, 1980, after an evening of heavy drinking, McInnes returned to his mother's home and committed suicide in the attic, cutting an artery with a razor blade.

Permission for an **exhumation** was obtained, and in February 1996, the grave that contained McInnes' body, and that of his mother, was opened. DNA samples were taken, as were samples from his surviving sister, Netta. The police also hoped to be able to compare a cast of his teeth with a bite mark on Helen Puttock's wrist.

For six months, Scottish forensic experts, together with members of the Department of Biological Anthropology at Cambridge University and the Institute of Forensic Medicine in Berlin, examined the samples obtained. Finally, the Lord Advocate of Scotland made the announcement: "Crown counsel have instructed that no further investigation is necessary in respect of John Irvine McInnes, and have concluded that, on the evidence available, criminal proceedings would not have been justified against Mr. McInnes."

The police apologized to McInnes' relatives for the distress of the exhumation and the publicity it had aroused, and Jeannie Williams declared that she was positive he was not the murderer of her sister-in-law.

Another suspect was proposed in October 2000. Ian Stephen, a psychologist who had worked on the Bible John case, now retired, told police that a man who was a relative of one of the prime suspects had contacted him. The suspect was the son of a Glasgow police officer, but had been brought up by an extremely religious aunt. In the late 1960s, his behavior had become strange, and he frequently stayed out all night. In 1970, he had suddenly put his house up for sale and moved south to England with his family. So far, he has not been found.

In February 1996, the grave that contained the bodies of John McInnes—considered a possible suspect—and his mother was opened. After extensive DNA analysis, it was announced that there was no evidence to connect McInnes with the murders, and the police publicly apologized to his surviving relatives.

The Vanished Lord

Belgravia, the area around Belgrave Square, is one of the most exclusive residential districts in London. But London streets, however upscale, frequently have a local "pub." Lower Belgrave Street is no exception, with its popular hostelry, the Plumber's Arms. At 9:45 P.M. on November 7, 1974, a small, slim woman burst through its doors, dressed only in a nightgown and covered with blood. "Help me, help me!" she screamed, "I have just escaped from a murderer! My children, my children—he is in my house, he has murdered the nanny!"

POLICE SEARCH THE MURDER SCENE

Locals immediately recognized the woman as Lady Veronica Lucan, the wife of Lord Richard Bingham, the Seventh Earl of Lucan. Within minutes, she was in nearby St. George's Hospital, treated for scalp wounds and shock, while police were on their way to her home at Number 46. Two uniformed officers found the front door of the house closed and, fearful for the safety of the children, smashed it open. There were no lights on inside, but the officers' flashlights revealed fresh bloodstains on the wall of the entrance hall and a pool of blood at the foot of the stairs. In a third-floor bedroom, a blood-soaked towel lay across the bed. On the floor above, they found the three children, scared but unharmed.

To complete their search of the premises, the policemen then went downstairs to the basement, where they discovered that the lamp had been removed from its socket and was lying on a nearby work surface. When they replaced it, signs of a violent struggle were revealed: more blood and

Left: Lord Richard Bingham announced his engagement to Veronica Duncan in October 1963. His father died shortly after the marriage, and he inherited the title of Seventh Earl of Lucan. However, he was soon to lose the family fortune as an addicted gambler.

The Plumbers Arms is a typical London local hostelry. It was through its doors that Lady Lucan staggered, dressed only in a nightgown and covered with blood. "Help me!" she cried. "I have just escaped from a murderer—he is in my house!"

the remains of broken teacups and saucers. And in the adjoining room stood a large canvas sack marked "U.S. Mail," with blood seeping through and the arm of a woman poking from its top.

The body of Sandra Rivett, the 29-year-old nanny to the children, had been thrust into the sack, doubled up, with her feet and head at the bottom. At first, the officers thought she might be alive, because her skin was still warm, but there was no detectable pulse.

Detectives arrived minutes later. In a room off the entrance hall, they found the murder weapon, a nine-inch length of lead pipe, matted with blood and hair. One end of the pipe had been bound with surgical tape, and the metal was deeply dented by the force of the blows that had been made with it. Next morning, although she was to remain in the hospital for six days, Lady Lucan was sufficiently recovered to make a formal statement to the police. The killer, she said confidently, was her husband.

A THEORY IS DEVELOPED

The police soon put forward a theory to explain the murder and Lucan's attack on his wife. He had, they suggested, decided to kill Lady Veronica, bundle the body into an inconspicuous old car he had borrowed from a friend, and drive to Newhaven on the south coast, where he kept a powerful

Lower Belgrave Street is in an exclusive residential district only a few hundred yards from Buckingham Palace. The Lucans and their three young children lived there until January 1973, when the earl stormed off to take up lone residence in a basement apartment in nearby Chelsea.

Sandra Rivett, aged 29, was the children's nanny. Married, but separated from her husband, she had worked only six weeks for the family before she was murdered. She was of similar build to Lady Lucan, and police surmised that, in the dark, Lord Lucan mistook her for his wife.

Lord Lucan at the wheel of his custom-built boat, *White Migrant,* at the start of the *Daily Express* international offshore powerboat race in August 1964. He had recently given up his job as a city banker and settled down to a life of sport and gambling.

speedboat. Then he would take the boat out into deep water and dispose of the corpse, weighted down with bricks or chains. After this, he would tell everybody that his deeply disturbed wife had disappeared, recover his children, and sell the house to pay his debts.

There was evidence that Lucan had hoped to establish an alibi. He booked a table for dinner at the Clermont Club and arrived there around

LORD LUCAN

Richard John Bingham, seventh Earl of Lucan, was born in 1934, the son of wealthy parents. His great-great-grandfather had been cavalry commander at Balaklava in 1854, during the Crimean War, when the Light Brigade had been destroyed in a

suicidal charge against the Russian guns. Richard married in 1963; shortly afterward, his father died, and he inherited the title, together with vast estates in England and Ireland.

The earl immediately gave up his job as a city banker and became a chronic gambler. An early win of £20,000 brought him the nickname of "Lucky Lucan," but his good fortune did not last. He gambled nearly every night at the Clermont Club, run by his friend John Aspinall, and within a few years had lost most of his inheritance and was selling off the family silver to pay his debts.

The marriage had been a stormy one from the beginning, and in January 1973, the couple parted, the earl going off to live alone in a basement apartment in nearby Chelsea. In May, he hired private detectives to snatch the three young children, and kept them in his apartment until ordered by a judge to return them to their mother. The custody fight cost him £40,000, and he was now in deeper debt than ever.

8:45 P.M. Then, the police suggested, he had secretly left the club, intending to return within an hour after committing the murder. But it all went disastrously wrong.

As far as Lucan knew, it was Sandra Rivett's night off. He let himself into the house with his key, put on gloves to avoid leaving fingerprints, and removed the lamp in the basement. Lurking in the dark, he intended to lure his wife downstairs, but it was the nanny who came. She was of much the same build as Lady Veronica, and in the dark, he could not see well, blindly lashing out again and again with the lead pipe, and then bundling the body into the mail sack. It was only when he heard his wife calling from above that he realized his mistake and ran upstairs to attack her. Perhaps he had exhausted his strength, perhaps his frenzy had spent itself, but, after raining seven blows on her head, he left her alive and fled from the house.

But where did Lucan go? Soon after leaving the murder scene, he telephoned his widowed mother, told her there had been a "terrible catastrophe," and asked her to go to care for the children. Later, near midnight, he suddenly arrived at the home of friends in Uckfield, in Sussex, halfway between London and Newhaven. He was disheveled and almost incoherent, with a large wet patch on the hip of his trousers. He said he had suffered "an unbelievable nightmare experience." He had been passing his wife's home when he looked through a window and saw a man attacking her. He had gone in to save her, but the attacker had escaped, and then his wife had run off into the night. Now, he said, he must drive back to London "to clear up the mess."

"MURDER, BY LORD LUCAN"

Next morning, the car that Lucan had borrowed was found in a parking lot at the docks in Newhaven. Bloodstains in the car matched the **blood groups** of Lady Lucan and Sandra Rivett. In the trunk was a length of lead pipe, bound with surgical tape, which had been cut from the murder weapon. And there was no sign of the speedboat. Two fishermen who had been preparing to go to sea early that morning reported that they saw a man who looked like Lucan on the small-craft jetty at Newhaven Harbor.

The police, via **Interpol**, radioed a message to other police forces, ports, and airports around the world with Lucan's description and requested his immediate arrest. However, although there were reports that he had been spotted in France, he ultimately vanished. The two detectives who led the hunt for the missing man were convinced that he had committed suicide, in shame and despair at the crime he had committed. They believed that he had taken the speedboat, from which he had intended to dump his wife's body, out to sea. There, possibly after weighting himself with the chains he had prepared to sink Lady Lucan's corpse, he had scuttled the boat. A former friend has even said that, during the summer of 1974, Lucan made two dummy runs in the boat, twice carrying out a sackful of bricks—the same weight of Lady Lucan—and dropping them into a deep area of the English Channel. Perhaps that is where Lord Lucan's body now lies.

Over the years, London's Scotland Yard has received hundreds of calls from people who claimed to have sighted Lucan, in almost every country in the world. But, as former Superintendent Drummond of the Murder Squad said in 1989, "There are dozens of ways he could have effectively changed his appearance without resorting to plastic surgery. He could have put on or lost weight dramatically. Even by growing a beard, dyeing his hair, wearing spectacles….Fifteen years on, the aging process would have changed him out of all recognition. He may have gone bald by now. His skin may be tanned dark brown and wrinkled."

Other detectives remain convinced that Lucan drowned himself in November. However, there is still a warrant for his arrest. At the inquest on Sandra Rivett's death in June 1975, the jury took only a few minutes to return the verdict: "Murder, by Lord Lucan."

IS HE STILL ALIVE?

Many of Lucan's gambling friends believed that he had escaped justice. One theory is that he somehow reached Southern Rhodesia (now Zimbabwe). There, under an alias, he exploited his military training—he was a former officer in the Guards—to join the Rhodesian army, which was then engaged in a bloody civil war. In 1987, a British newspaper, under the headline "Lucan Lives!," reported that he was living "somewhere in southern Africa." Other people believe that he reached Australia, or even New Zealand, where he lives to this day, under an assumed name, as a sheep farmer or cattle rancher. Finally, there is the grisly rumor that he in fact committed suicide, and his body was discovered by friends and fed to the tigers that John Aspinall kept in his private zoo.

WANTED

SAN FRANCISCO POLICE DEPARTMENT

ORIGINAL DRAWING

AMENDED DRAWING

Supplementing our Bulletin 87-69 of October 13, 1969. Additional information has developed the above amended drawing of murder suspect known as "ZODIAC".

WMA, 35-45 Years, approximately 5'8", Heavy Build, Short Brown Hair, possibly with Red Tint, Wears Glasses. Armed with 9 MM Automatic.

Available for comparison: Slugs, Casings, Latents, Handwriting.

ANY INFORMATION:
Inspectors Armstrong & Toschi
Homicide Detail
CASE NO. 696314

THOMAS J. CAHILL
CHIEF OF POLICE

Zodiac

Between October 30, 1966, and December 2, 1973, more than 40 people, mainly young women, were violently attacked in California. Only three persons survived, and it has been suggested that all were the victims of one man, who came to be known as the "Zodiac Killer." He has never been found. The first death was that of Cheri Jo Bates, an 18-year-old freshman at Riverside City College near Los Angeles. She came out of the campus library to find that her car would not start: the distributor coil had been disconnected. Her killer approached and dragged her behind some nearby bushes, where he stabbed and slashed her so violently that her head was nearly severed from her body. A few days later, a letter to the local newspaper declared, "Cheri is not the first and she will not be the last." The following April, identical letters were received by the newspapers, the police, and Cheri's father. They stated: "Bates had to die. There will be more."

MORE KILLINGS

More than 18 months passed before the killer struck again. Late in the evening of December 20, 1968, 17-year-old David Faraday parked his car off the road near Lake Herman, above Vallejo, on the north side of San Francisco Bay. Beside him sat pretty, 16-year-old Betty Lou Jensen. A short time later, a night-stalking gunman came upon them and shot David point-blank as he sat at the wheel of the car. Betty Lou ran 10 yards before she was gunned down with five shots in the back from a .22-caliber automatic pistol. Police were confounded: there were no witnesses, no motive. The

Left: On October 11, 1969, a San Francisco cab driver was shot dead with a gun used, as proven later, in two previous "Zodiac" murders. A police artist produced a drawing of the wanted man, based on witnesses' descriptions, and then modified it after further questioning of the witnesses.

Three of Zodiac's victims. From left to right: Paul Stine, San Francisco cab driver shot in the head; coed Cecilia Shepard, stabbed 14 times and killed; and her former boyfriend Bryan Hartnell, who was stabbed five times and left for dead, but survived to give police a partial description.

only possible suspect, a boy who had been "bugging" Betty Lou at school and who had threatened to beat up David, had a solid alibi.

On July 4, 1969, 19-year-old Michael Mageau took his date, 22-year-old Darlene Ferrin, for an evening drive. At one point, Michael believed they were being followed by another car, but Darlene seemed to know the other driver and told him, "Don't worry about it." Shortly before midnight, they parked in a lot less than 2 miles (3 km) from the spot where David and Betty Lou had been murdered. They had been there around 10 minutes when a man stepped out of the shadows, walked up to the car, shone a flashlight inside, and started shooting without saying a word. Darlene was hit several times in the chest and died instantly. Michael took a bullet in the neck, which shattered his jaw and tore away part of his tongue; other shots wounded him in the leg, elbow, and shoulder. The gunman left him for dead, but he survived.

"I WANT TO REPORT A DOUBLE MURDER"

An hour after the shooting, the Vallejo Police Department received a call from a pay phone. A soft voice announced: "I want to report a double murder. If you will go one mile east on Columbia Parkway to the public park, you will find kids in a brown car. They were shot with a 9-millimeter Luger. I also killed those kids last year. Goodbye." The police traced the call and learned that a "stocky" man had been seen using the phone at that time. However, that was the only clue they had.

Talking about the murder later, Darlene's friends recalled that she had been receiving anonymous phone calls and threatening visits from a heavyset stranger in the preceding weeks. She referred to the man as "Paul" and told her babysitter: "He doesn't want anyone to know what I saw him do. I saw him murder someone."

After the July 4, 1969, shooting, Zodiac telephoned the Vallejo Police Department and said, "I want to report a double murder." He announced that he had shot two youngsters with a 9-millimeter Luger, an automatic pistol of the type illustrated here.

The police were unable to identify "Paul," and had to add the killing to their list of unsolved murders. Then, on August 1, the editors of the Vallejo *Times-Herald,* the San Francisco *Examiner,* and the *San Francisco Chronicle,* each received a letter, signed with a cross over a circle. This, it was guessed, was a zodiac symbol, although it was also ominously similar to a gun sight.

The letter was crudely written and badly spelled. It began: "Dear Editor This is the murderer of the 2 teenagers last Christmass at Lake Herman & the girl on the 4th of July near the golf course in Vallejo To prove I killed them I shall state some facts which only I & the police know." Indeed, the details were sufficient to make it clear that the writer was definitely the killer. With the letters, each newspaper received one third of a message in **cipher**, a set of random symbols with no obvious meaning. The killer's letter concluded:

"I want you to print this cipher on the front page of your newspaper. In this cipher is my identity. If you do not print this cipher by the afternoon of Fry. 1st of Aug 69, I will go on a kill Ram-page Fry. night. I will cruse around all weekend killing lone people in the night then move on to kill again, until I end up with a dozen people over the weekend."

The newspapers wisely published the pieces of the cipher message. Six days later, a three-page letter arrived. It began, "This is the Zodiac

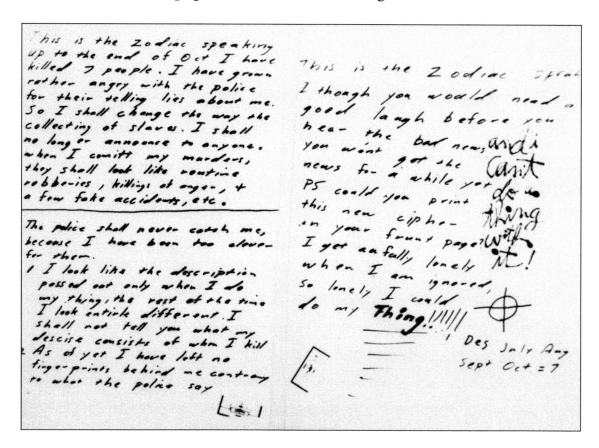

Part of the three-page letter sent to the San Francisco *Examiner*. It began, "This is the Zodiac speaking," and continued: "In answer to your asking for more details about the good times I had in Vallejo, I shall be happy to provide them with even more material...."

THE ZODIAC CIPHER

Each one-third of the cipher message consisted of eight lines of 17 symbols. Naval Intelligence, the CIA, and NSA said they were unable to interpret it, probably because it was too unsophisticated. Donald Harden, a teacher at North Salinas High School, and his wife broke it in a day and a half. It was a simple substitution cipher, and read:

"I like killing people because it is so much fun it is more fun than killing wild game in the forrest because man is the most dangerous anamal of all to kill something gives me the most thrilling experence it is even better than getting your rocks off with a girl the best part of it is thae when i die i will be reborn in paradice and thei i have killed will become my slaves i will not give you my name because you will try to sloi down or atop my collectiog of slaves for afterlife ebeorietemethhpitti." It is obvious that, even with his substitution table beside him, the killer had made several mistakes.

speaking," and gave further details of the Vallejo killings, explaining that the murderer had been able to see his bloody work by taping a pencil flashlight to the barrel of his gun.

The police were no nearer identifying Zodiac, and on September 27, he struck again. This time, Bryan Hartnell, 20, and Cecilia Shephard, 22, were having a picnic at Lake Berryessa, near Vallejo. A hooded gunman approached them and told them he was an escaped convict. He tied them up with rope and then stabbed Bryan five times and Cecilia 14 times. Bryan survived, but Cecilia was found dead. Before he left, the gunman scribbled a note on the door of Bryan's car. It read: "Vallejo 12-20-68, 7-4-69, Sept 27-69-6:30 by knife."

"School children make nice targets, I think I shall wipe out a school bus some morning," wrote Zodiac. His threat provoked panic among parents in the Bay Area.

On October 11, a San Francisco cab driver was shot in the head and killed with a 9-mm pistol, and **ballistics** tests showed it was the same gun used to kill David Faraday and Betty Lou Jensen. Following this, Zodiac sent a succession of letters, some of which contained pieces of the victim's bloodstained shirt. In one, he wrote: "School children make nice targets, I think I shall wipe out a school bus some morning. Just shoot out the front tire & then pick off the kiddies as they come bouncing out." In another, he claimed seven murders, rather than the five attributed to him by police.

There was a sensational development on October 22, when a man claiming to be Zodiac called the police in Oakland. He said he wanted to speak to one of two top criminal lawyers on the following morning's Channel 7 talk show. Famous attorney Melvin Belli agreed to appear. When the man called, he had a series of long conversations on air with the lawyer and told him he suffered from blinding headaches. Finally, he agreed to meet Belli in front of a store in Daly City, but, predictably, he failed to turn up. Eventually, the caller was traced to Napa State Hospital and was found to be a mental patient there. He was certainly not Zodiac.

A CLOSE CALL FOR MOTHER AND BABY

In November, the editor of the *San Francisco Chronicle* received a commercially printed greeting card. On its front were a picture of a dripping fountain pen and the message, "Sorry I haven't written, but I just washed my pen...." Inside, together with another cipher text, Zodiac had scribbled the words "and I can't do a thing with it!" There was also a threat to bomb a bus, with a rough sketch to show how it would be detonated.

In the weeks that followed, there were two more unexplained killings,

The envelope that enclosed the Christmas card sent by Zodiac to attorney Melvin Belli, in which he made a plea for help: "I am finding it extreamly difficult to hold it in check." It also contained a piece of bloodstained shirt, identified as having been torn from one of his victims.

In an enclosed phone booth at the studios of KGO-TV in San Francisco, Melvin Belli takes a call from a man claiming to be Zodiac. The man agreed to meet Belli in Daly City, but failed to turn up, and was later traced as a mental patient at Napa State Hospital.

WAS HE ZODIAC?

A cartoonist on the *San Francisco Chronicle* named Robert Graysmith wrote a book in 1986, which was a detailed study of the Zodiac murders. He claimed that the killer was a man he called "Robert Hall Starr." His erratic behavior early in 1971 caused his family to wonder whether he just might be Zodiac and, eventually, they informed the police of their suspicions.

"Starr" was a loner who collected rifles and hunted game and could be said to resemble the rough descriptions of the killer. The only positive clue held by the police was a set of fingerprints found in the cab of Paul Stine; these did not match the suspect's in any way, however, and the investigation went no further. But Graysmith's talks with police officers, and with those who knew "Starr," convinced him of the killer's identity. And the most telling piece of circumstantial evidence was that in the period from 1974–78, when no Zodiac letters were sent, "Starr" had spent three years committed to an institution for child molesting.

although the police were unsure that these were attributable to Zodiac. Then Melvin Belli received a Christmas card, pleading for help: "I am finding it extreamly difficult to hold it in check I am afraid I will lose control again and take my nineth & possibly tenth victim."

On March 22, 1970, Kathleen Johns and her 10-month-old baby daughter were offered a ride to a service station near Modesto by a man who told her that the rear tire on her car was loose. Instead, he drove her away through a maze of winding roads, calmly remarking every now and then: "You know I'm going to kill you." Miraculously, the driver drove onto the exit ramp of a freeway by mistake, and, as he stopped, Mrs. Johns was able to jump from the car with her baby and take refuge in an irrigation

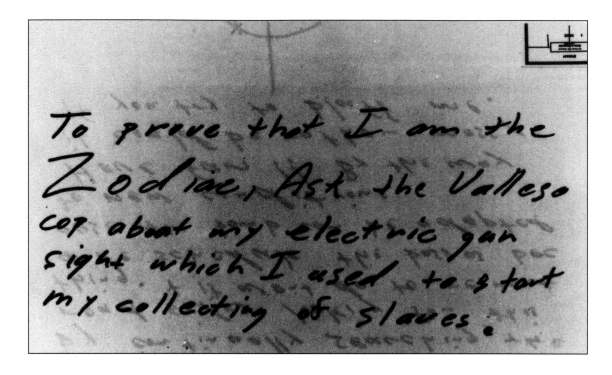

Part of a seven-page letter received by the *San Francisco Chronicle* on November 9, 1969. Zodiac announced that he covered his fingertips with glue, so as not to leave prints. The letter included a description, and a crudely drawn diagram of a bomb that he planned to use.

ditch. When she was later able to reach a police station, she noticed an artist's composite portrait of Zodiac on a "Wanted" poster. "That's him!" she cried. "That's him right there!" And she was able to give the first detailed description of the killer.

"I AM BACK WITH YOU"

Nine more letters were sent by Zodiac between April 1970 and March 1971. There were four or five unexplained killings in this period, but police were sure that at least one was a "copy cat" crime. In one letter, claiming his tenth victim, Zodiac wrote: "It would have been a lot more except that my bus bomb was a dud. I was swamped out by the rain we had a while back."

After this, newspaper journalists and police officers continued to receive letters, most of which were judged to be hoaxes. However, unsolved murders still occurred for several years in the San Francisco Bay

ZODIAC IN NEW YORK?

In the summer of 1990, Jerry Nachman, editor of the *New York Post*, received a letter signed with the Zodiac symbol, giving details of three men shot, but not killed, in Brooklyn in March through May. They had all been shot, determined ballistics experts, with a low-quality firearm, a "Saturday night special," or a "zip-gun," loaded with .38- or 9-mm-caliber bullets. However, the assailant was described as a black man, although one of the surviving victims said he had been wearing a brown ski mask and gloves.

New York police requested the closed file on Zodiac from Sacramento, and a few days later, the *Post* announced that handwriting analysis showed that New York's Zodiac was not San Francisco's. However, following the wounding of a sleeping homeless man in Central Park on June 21, the newspaper received another letter that claimed, "It is one of the same Zodiac one Zodiac." But there were no further similar attacks, and in October, the case file was closed.

area, and in January 1974, the *San Francisco Chronicle* received a Zodiac letter that was considered genuine, ending with the score: "Me-37 SFPD-0." Then, for four years, nothing more was heard, until, on April 25, 1978, a letter arrived at the *Chronicle* with the chilling message, "I am back with you."

Police speculated that during this period the killer might have been in prison on an unrelated charge or even receiving treatment in a mental institution. Perhaps significantly, in the light of the 1969 Christmas card to Melvin Belli, the letter ended, "I am now in control of all things." And there were no further killings attributed to Zodiac in California.

Karen Silkwood

*The unexplained death of 28-year-old chemical technician Karen Silkwood on November 13, 1974, has provoked a great deal of controversy in the United States, and became the subject of a major motion picture starring Meryl Streep. It has continued to raise questions about the safety of employees in the nuclear industry, as well as persistent accusations that Karen was murdered because "she knew too much." On the evening of her death, she was on her way to meet a reporter from **The New York Times**, intending to hand over the evidence she had gathered.*

RADIOACTIVE GLOVE BOX

Karen worked at the Kerr-McGee plutonium fuels production plant in Crescent, Oklahoma, and was an active member of the Oil, Chemical & Atomic Workers' Union. She worked in the metallography laboratory, using a "glove box." This is a supposedly sealed environment into which she inserted her hands through radioactive-proof gloves to grind and polish plutonium pellets for use in fuel rods for nuclear-power reactors. Over time, she became concerned about working conditions in the plant. She maintained that safety records were routinely falsified. There were rumors that radioactive contamination was regularly detected and that significant quantities of plutonium were "disappearing" and unaccounted for.

In October 1974, Karen told a union representative that the welds in the stainless-steel tubes to hold the plutonium pellets were below the required standard—"out of tolerance, no matter what they look like"—and that

Left: Meryl Streep as Karen Silkwood in the movie made about her life, which also starred Kurt Russell (far left). The case of Karen Silkwood raised major concerns about the health and safety of America's nuclear workers.

Meryl Streep as Karen Silkwood in another scene from the movie made of Karen's life, with Cher portraying one of Karen's friends listening to her concerns about safety at the Kerr-McGee plutonium fuels production plant in Oklahoma.

PLUTONIUM

Plutonium is a heavy silver-white metallic element. Minute quantities have occasionally been found in radioactive ores, but it can be manufactured artificially by bombarding uranium 238 with neutrons in a nuclear reactor. Plutonium is important, not only for nuclear weapons, but also for its employment in "super-reactors," the experimental use for which it was intended in the tubes manufactured by Kerr-McGee. The element is extremely dangerous, not so much for its radioactivity outside the body, but in cases in which it is absorbed. Plutonium enters the cells of the lungs, liver, and blood, where internal radiation can prove fatal.

X-ray photographs showing the acceptability of the welds were regularly retouched. In the week before her death, Karen was reportedly gathering evidence for the union to support her claims that the maintenance of safety in the Kerr-McGee plant was negligent.

RADIOACTIVE CONTAMINATION

A week before, halfway through her work on the evening of November 5, Karen decided to monitor herself for radioactive contamination, using the detector that was mounted beside the glove box. The right side of her coveralls, mostly the sleeve and shoulder, gave an unexpectedly high reading. She at once reported to the plant's Health Physics Office, where she was given a "nasal swipe." This was a test to measure a person's exposure to airborne plutonium, and could also indicate that plutonium had been transferred from a person's hands to his or her nose. It gave a small positive indication, but nowhere near as much as that on her coveralls.

Karen was put through a complete decontamination cleanup, and both gloves in the glove box were replaced. It was said that no leaks were found in the removed gloves, although, strangely, plutonium contamination was found on the surfaces that had been in contact with Karen's hands. A check on the surfaces of the metallography laboratory allegedly found no contamination, and the filters from two air monitors in the room did not reveal any plutonium in the air. After three hours, Karen returned to work, but did no further work in the glove box. When she left the plant after midnight, she once again monitored herself and reported that she was clean. As a further precautionary measure, however, she was put on a program in which all her urine and feces were to be collected for **bioassay** over the next five days.

The following morning, Karen returned to work. She was engaged in paperwork for an hour, but did not use the glove box, and then left the laboratory for a meeting. As she went, she monitored herself and found significant contamination on her hands. At the Health Physics Office, staff found further radioactivity on her right forearm and the right side of her neck and face, and she was given decontamination treatment. She then asked a technician to check out her locker and car, but no activity was detected in either.

KAREN'S APARTMENT IS CHECKED

The next day, Karen reported to the Health Physics Office with her first set of samples for bioassay. They revealed extremely high levels of radioactivity, and lower—but significant—levels were found on her hands, arms, chest, neck, and right ear. Once again, her locker and car were checked, with negative results.

After Karen had been thoroughly cleaned up, technicians accompanied her to her apartment, which she shared with another laboratory worker, Sherri Ellis. In the bathroom, extremely high levels of radioactivity were found on the toilet seat and the floor, where Karen had spilled a few drops of her urine sample that morning. In the kitchen, even higher levels were

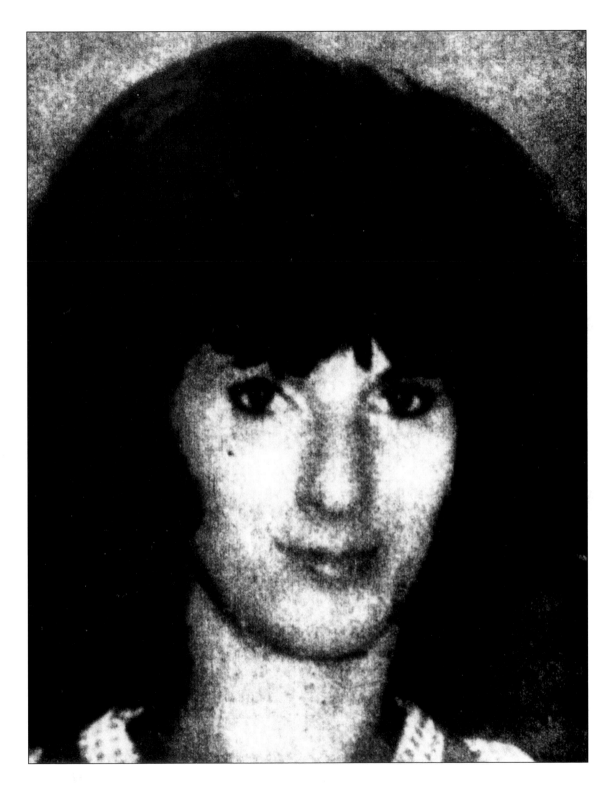

This undated file photograph of Karen Silkwood shows the brave young woman who died in the most mysterious of circumstances after raising concerns about safety at the giant Kerr-McGee plutonium plant in Oklahoma. In 1983, the estate of Karen Silkwood won a Supreme Court battle and was awarded $10.5 million against the company.

THE QUAALUDE ANALYSIS

The sedative methaqualone is commonly known as Quaalude. The report on Karen's autopsy stated that blood tests showed 0.35 milligrams of the drug per 100 milliliters of blood and an additional 50 milligrams undissolved in her stomach. There are approximately 5 liters of blood in the body, indicating 17.5 milligrams of methaqualone in Karen's blood, and a total of 67.5 milligrams, mostly unabsorbed.

Medical textbooks give the normal single dose of methaqualone as 75 milligrams (although tablets of 150 milligrams were regularly dispensed before the prescription of Quaalude was discontinued) and the expected blood level as 0.5 per 100 milliliters. It seems likely, then, that Karen, understandably agitated after her experiences and her union meeting, had taken perhaps a half-tablet to settle her nerves before the coming encounter with the *Times* reporter. However, it would hardly have been enough to cause her to lose control of the car.

detected, particularly on a package of bologna and cheese that she had handled. Plutonium was also detected on her bed linen, but only at a low level. Sherri Ellis was also found to be slightly contaminated and was immediately returned to the Kerr-McGee plant to be cleaned up.

The detection of so much plutonium in Karen and Sherri's apartment raised serious questions. The two women, and Karen's boyfriend, Drew Stephens, were therefore sent to Los Alamos National Laboratory, New Mexico, for further testing. On the following day, Dr. George Voelz, the leader of the laboratory's Health Division, had good news for Sherri and Drew: the level of plutonium in their bodies was slight, but insignificant.

Karen, on the other hand, had nearly half the maximum allowable amount of plutonium in her lungs. However, Dr. Voelz assured her that, based on his experience of nuclear fuel workers with even greater amounts of plutonium in their bodies, she should not be fearful of dying from radiation poisoning or of developing cancer. Karen, nevertheless, was deeply concerned. She asked whether the plutonium would affect her ability to have children or cause her children to be deformed. Dr. Voelz gave her such reassurances as he could.

The three returned home on November 12, and the next morning, Karen and Sherri reported for work, but they were temporarily withdrawn from any handling of radioactive materials. After work, Karen attended a meeting of her union, at which she spoke of her concern about safety

A press conference held by the Supporters of Silkwood in 1984. Kitty Tucker, who founded the organization to back the Silkwood family's civil suit and demand further investigation, is speaking. Father William Davis, one of the supporters, sits listening at Kitty's right.

After Silkwood's death, concern for the safety of workers in the nuclear power industry increased. A distinguished panel led a "teach-in" protest in 1979. They included consumer advocate Ralph Nader and Sara Nelson of the Karen Silkwood Fund (respectively first and second from left).

conditions at the plant. At the end of the meeting, about 7:00 P.M., she left alone in her car, on her way to meet the *Times* reporter.

THE UNANSWERED QUESTIONS

At 8:05 P.M., Karen was found dead in her car, seven miles (11 km) from the Kerr-McGee plant. The car had crashed off the road, and she had died of multiple injuries. An Oklahoma State trooper reported that the crash had not involved another vehicle and was typical of the driver having fallen asleep at the wheel. Because of this, no homicide inquiry was made.

Karen's father, Bill Silkwood, speaking to reporters outside the federal courthouse in Oklahoma City in 1979, following a civil suit brought against Kerr-McGee for negligence contributory to Karen's death. The court had just awarded $10.5 million for personal injury.

These are spent nuclear pellets, which form radioactive atomic waste. Karen Silkwood claimed that pellets similar to these were of a poor standard and causing radioactive contamination at the Kerr-McGee plant where they were produced.

However, subsequent private investigations requested by her attorneys revealed fresh dents and traces of rubber on the rear fender of the car, suggesting that Karen had been forced off the road. Furthermore, the documentary evidence that she had been taking to her meeting with the reporter was never found.

The Oklahoma State medical examiner, Dr. A. Jay Chapman, was unwilling to perform an autopsy on a body reportedly contaminated with plutonium, and a team was therefore sent from Los Alamos to carry out the examination at the University Hospital, Oklahoma City. They found quantities of plutonium in the body consistent with those discovered when Karen was alive. Supporting the theory that she had fallen asleep at the wheel of her car, the autopsy allegedly found twice the normal dose of Quaalude (a **sedative**) in her body. Later analysis of Karen's lungs at Los Alamos indicated that she had been exposed to heavy contamination within the month before her death.

There are questions that have never been answered. How did Karen Silkwood become exposed to such contamination, and what was its source? Is it true that she was subjected to extreme harassment by Kerr-McGee executives because of her protests against poor safety standards at the plant? And how did her car come to leave the road? Was she followed by someone who rear-ended the car and then took incriminating paperwork from the wreckage? And why were authorities so anxious to imply that she had fallen asleep while driving?

Karen's estate filed a civil suit against Kerr-McGee. When the trial ended in 1979, the jury awarded $10.5 million for personal injury and **punitive** damages. However, the Federal Court of Appeals, in Denver, Colorado, reversed the verdict, allowing a mere $5,000 for personal property lost during the decontamination of the apartment. It was not until 1986, 12 years after Karen's death, that the suit was set for retrial, but it was then finally settled out of court for $1.3 million. The Kerr-McGee plant closed in 1975.

CHANDRA LEVY

Every year in the United States, thousands of adults are reported "missing" by their families, friends, work associates, or (in the case of wanted criminals) the police. All these persons are missing, either because they wish completely to sever relations with those around them, have committed suicide, are suffering from amnesia, or because they are victims—either of abduction or of homicide. A recent case that provoked huge media interest was that of Chandra Levy.

Chandra was a 24-year-old intern in the U.S. Bureau of Prisons in Washington, D.C., who went missing on April 30, 2001. The case generated national attention because Democrat Congressman Gary Condit, who represents the area of California that includes her home town of Modesto, admitted to investigators that he was having an affair with her—a circumstance that led to his being considered a possible suspect.

It was discovered that Chandra had downloaded information from the Internet about a historic house in Rock Creek Park, northwest of the city, shortly before her disappearance. Immediately, the police conducted a detailed search of the park, but reported they could find no trace of the missing woman—although they uncovered some 25 animal bones. They later extended their search to three parks southwest of the city, but drew a blank in every one.

Mr. Condit came under intense pressure during the early days of the investigation, which dragged on for many months. Then, on May 22, 2002, after 13 months, parts of a human skeleton were discovered in Rock Creek Park by a man walking his dog and identified as those of Chandra Levy. Three weeks later, two small bones from the left foot and a left thigh bone were also discovered. Dr Jonathan Arden, Washington, D.C.'s medical examiner, said "they were completely consistent with the other bones." It was presumed that the bones had been scattered by marauding animals.

Private investigators hired by Chandra's parents also found some twisted wire, which has been turned over to the FBI to be examined for any evidence that it might have been used in an attack on her. Police said it appeared to be the same that was used by park workers to secure trees, but the assistant superintendent said that they used a heavier gauge wire and ran it through sections of garden hose to avoid damaging the bark.

GLOSSARY

Acquit: to discharge completely from an accusation

Alibi: the plea of having been elsewhere than at the place where a certain act was committed

Autopsy: the detailed examination of a dead body in order to determine cause of death

Ballistics: the study of the processes within a firearm as it is fired

Bioassay: chemical analysis of biological samples

Blood group: one of four main types of blood: A, B, AB, and O; every person has blood of one particular group, and blood of one group will cause clotting if mixed with another, so it is easy to distinguish the group and the person from which it came

Cipher: a set of symbols, each of which represents a number or a letter of the alphabet

Circumstantial evidence: evidence that can contribute to the conviction of an accused person, but that is not considered sufficient without eyewitness or forensic evidence

Commute: to change a penalty to another one less severe

Embezzlement: taking money for one's own use in violation of trust

Exhumation: to take a body out of its grave or tomb

Garrote: to strangle someone using a thin wire with handles at either end

Interpol: an association of national police forces that promotes cooperation and mutual assistance in apprehending international criminals and criminals who flee abroad to avoid justice.

Parole: a conditional release of a prisoner serving an indeterminate or unexpired sentence

Punitive: aimed at punishment

Racketeering: the branch of organized crime that obtains money by fraud or extortion

Scuttle: to cut a hole through the bottom, deck, or side of a ship

Sedative: a drug that has a calming or tranquilizing effect

CHRONOLOGY

1913:	James Riddle Hoffa is born in Brazil, Indiana.
1924:	Elizabeth Short is born in Boston, Massachusetts.
1934:	Richard John Bingham is born in England.
1942:	"Beth" Short's first time in California.
1945:	Beth Short returns to California and is nicknamed "Black Dahlia."
1946:	Karen Silkwood is born in Longview, Texas.
1947:	January 8, "Black Dahlia" is found murdered in Los Angeles.
1957:	Hoffa becomes president of the Teamsters Union.
1963:	Bingham marries, later inherits title Earl of Lucan.
1964:	Hoffa is convicted of jury tampering.
1966:	October 30, Cheri Jo Bates is murdered in Riverside, California; she is the first "Zodiac" killing.
1968:	December 20, David Faraday and Betty Lou Jensen are murdered in Vallejo, California.
1969:	July 4, Darlene Ferrin is murdered in Vallejo; August 1, first "Zodiac" letters are received; September 27, Cecilia Shepherd is murdered; October 11, cab driver Paul Stine is murdered in San Francisco.
1970:	March 22, Kathleen Johns escapes "Zodiac Killer" in Modesto, California.
1971:	Hoffa's prison sentence is commuted.
1972:	Karen Silkwood is employed at Kerr-McGee plant, Crescent, Oklahoma.
1973:	Lord Lucan abducts his three children.

1974:   November 7, Sandra Rivett is murdered; Lord Lucan disappears; November 13, Karen Silkwood is killed in Oklahoma.

1975:   July 30, Jimmy Hoffa disappears.

1978:   April 25, last confirmed "Zodiac" letter is received.

1990:   Four men are wounded in a shooting; assailant claims to be "Zodiac."

FURTHER INFORMATION

Useful Web Sites

www.pbs.org/wgbh/pages/frontline

detnews.com/history/hoffa/hoffa

www.lordlucan.com

www.parmaq.com/truecrime/Lucan

www.crimelibrary.com/zodiac

www.bethshort.com

Further Reading

Gould, Russell. *Unsolved Murders.* London: Virgin, 2001.

Graysmith, Robert. *Zodiac.* New York: St. Martin's Press, 1976.

Jeffries, Paul H. *Who Killed Precious?* Boston: Little, Brown, 1991.

Kohn, Howard. *Who Killed Karen Silkwood?* New York: Simon & Schuster, 1981.

Marnham, Patrick. *The Trail of Havoc—In the Steps of Lord Lucan.* New York: Viking Press, 1988.

Newton, Michael. *Hunting Humans.* New York: Avon Books, 1992.

Powell, Phelan. *Major Unsolved Crimes.* Philadelphia, PA: Chelsea House Publishers, 2000.

Smith, Ken. *Raw Deal.* New York: Blast Books, 1998.

Wilson, Kirk. *Unsolved Crimes.* London: Robinson, 2002.

About the Author

Dr. Brian Innes has been writing on criminal subjects since 1966, when he began work on a series that included *The Book of Pirates, The Book of Spies,* and *The Book of Outlaws.* After contributing to the weekly publication *The Unsolved,* he provided a long series on forensic science, as well as a number of feature articles for *Real Life Crimes,* and his book, *Crooks and Conmen,* was published in 1992.

He has also written *The History of Torture* (1998); *Death and the Afterlife* (1999); and *Bodies of Evidence* (2000), a detailed study of forensic science. He has also contributed commentary for a History Channel feature on punishment. A graduate scientist, Dr. Innes spent a number of years in industry as a research biochemist, and has written extensively on scientific topics, notably for the Marshall-Cavendish *Encyclopedia of Science.* He now lives, and continues his writing, in a converted watermill and former iron forge in southern France.

INDEX